Coping Skills for Kids Activity Books: Processing Feelings
Copyright © 2019 by Janine Halloran, LMHC

For information, contact:
Coping Skills for Kids/Encourage Play, LLC
288 Grove Street #321
Braintree, MA 02184
http://www.copingskillsforkids.com

Illustration by Meg Garcia at Mabel Bean & Co

ISBN: 978-1-7333871-2-5

First Edition: September 2019
10 9 8 7 6 5 4 3 2 1

Coping Skills for Kids

ACTIVITY BOOKS™

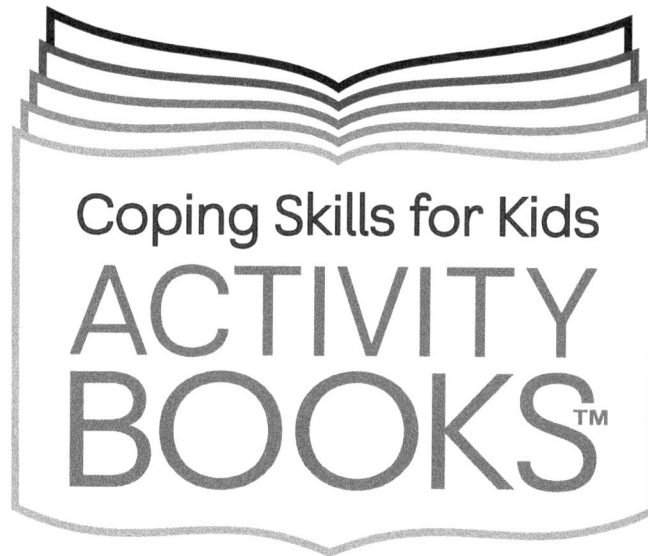

Processing
FEELINGS

Written by Janine Halloran, LMHC
Illustrated by Meg Garcia

"Feelings are mentionable and manageable"
- Fred Rogers

Contents

How To Use The Processing Feelings Activity Book

The activities in this book are designed to help kids explore their feelings. We cover ten of the most common feelings kids have a hard time expressing and provide blank worksheets kids can fill in with any feelings they want.

Feelings included are:

Sad
Frustrated
Mad
Worried
Anxious

Embarrassed
Scared
Overwhelmed
Stressed
Jealous

Activities included are:

The _____ Feelings Thermometer

The ability to identify not only *what* you are feeling, but also *how much* you are feeling, is an essential piece of managing your emotions, thoughts, and behaviors. If kids recognize the beginning of a more significant reaction to a situation, they can intervene and use the right coping skill to help self-manage their feelings. The goal is for kids to use a coping skill when they are lower on the thermometer, *before* things escalate.

The other benefit of the Feelings Thermometer is that it helps kids match feelings and coping skills together.

To learn how to fill out the thermometer, let's use "mad" as an example.

1. Ask the child to pick out three colors and designate one color for each section of the thermometer. For example, yellow for the bottom, orange for the middle and red for the top.

2. Ask the child think about what they look like when they're just a little bit mad (at the bottom of the thermometer). Like, "Do you sigh loudly? Do you growl and make a face?"

3. Moving on to the middle section, ask the child what medium-sized mad looks like. "Does your voice get louder? Do you stomp your feet?"

4. Finally, ask what being VERY mad looks like. "Is it yelling or throwing things?"

5. Once you identify *behaviors* on the thermometer together, work on identifying *coping skills* the child can use to calm down. Some examples include getting a cold drink of water, taking deep breaths, doing push ups, or squeezing play dough. (For more ideas, the Coping Skills for Kids Cue Cards™ offer 40+ skills per deck, organized by Relaxation, Movement, Processing, Distraction, and Sensory in order for children to choose what best fits their personality and the situation.)

What makes you feel _____?

Sometimes it's hard for kids to express themselves just by talking. This worksheet is an opportunity for kids to write or draw what makes them feel different emotions.

What makes other people feel _____?

Some kids struggle to identify their own feelings. An easier way to start the conversation is to begin by asking about other people's feelings instead.

Pick one color and draw about feeling _____.

Kids can express themselves by picking a color that connects to a feeling and then drawing about that feeling using the color. For example, some kids may use grey for sad or yellow for happy.

Draw about feeling _____ using shapes.

Using shapes is another way for kids to share and express their feelings. For example, some kids may draw sad as raindrop shapes, or happy as hearts.

Draw or write coping skills you can use when you feel _____.

The goal of Coping Skills for Kids™ is to help children identify safe and healthy coping skills they can use when experiencing different emotions. This activity helps kids start to make the connection between having a feeling and using an appropriate coping skill to express or manage that feeling safely.

How are you feeling today? Draw or write about it.

At the end of the book, these worksheets are a way to start a dialogue with kids about their in-the-moment feelings by using writing or drawing instead of talking out loud.

A Note for Parents and Caregivers

The activities in this workbook are designed to help you get a better understanding of the things that may be causing your child to feel the way they do. Often, children will share ideas in writing or in drawing that they may not have the words for or feel comfortable saying out loud. Approaching big feelings in a variety of ways may unlock conversation: the right key may allow your child to open up and give you a deeper understanding of their inner world.

It can be hard for kids to explore their feelings, so they may need extra support from a parent or a trusted adult to benefit from the exercises fully.

This is not a book that your child has to do in order or finish in one day. For example, your child doesn't have to complete all the sad worksheets first, then the frustrated ones, etc. Do what works for your child. You can better ease into conversations if you start with feelings they are more comfortable talking about first, then move on to the emotions they are having a hard time expressing safely, so use your best judgment. Have them take their time, and use the worksheets as a jumping-off point for discussions about feelings.

To help a child build their emotional skills, we need to work with them when they are able to hear us and take in information. The best time to do that is when they are calm, not when they are in crisis.

Worksheets can be used as a follow-up after a challenging situation. For example, let's say your child got very mad about something earlier in the day and is now calm, but having a hard time sharing in words what happened. Your child can use the "How am I feeling today?" page to share more about what was happening.

Also, feel free to share your own thoughts and feelings with your child. You have feelings, too! They love to hear stories about what makes you feel specific ways. This also opens up the door for you to share some of your healthy ways of coping with big feelings.

The completed book will serve as a valuable reference guide to your child when situations arise in the future!

A Note for Professionals

The activities in this book are designed to help everyone get a better understanding of the things that may be causing a child to feel the way they do. Often, kids will share ideas in writing or in drawing that they may not have the words for or feel comfortable saying out loud. Approaching the same feeling in a variety of ways allows us to get a deeper understanding of their inner world.

This is not a book that your student or client has to do in order, or must finish all in one day. Do what works for the child you have in front of you. It can ease you into conversations if you start with more comfortable feelings first, then move on to the emotions they are having a hard time expressing safely. Use your best judgment. Have them take their time and use the worksheets as a jumping-off point for discussions.

To help a child build their emotional skills, we need to work with them when they are able to hear us and take in information. The best time to do that is when they are calm, not when they are in crisis.

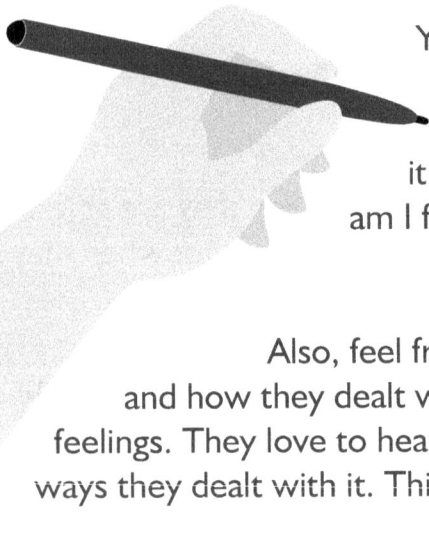

You may use the book as a follow-up after a challenging situation. For example, let's say a child got very stressed earlier in the school day. They have calmed down, but they are finding it hard to share in words what happened. They can use the "How am I feeling today?" page as an opportunity to share more about what was happening for them.

Also, feel free to share real-world examples of people experiencing feelings and how they dealt with it. Kids desperately want to know they are not alone in their feelings. They love to hear stories about others who have experienced similar feelings and ways they dealt with it. This is also an opportunity to share healthy coping strategies you've seen work for others.

There's more online!

www.copingskillsforkids.com

Books and products in the collection:

Coping Skills for Kids Coping Cue Cards™ series:
The Discovery Deck
The Relaxation Deck
The Distraction Deck
The Movement Deck
The Sensory Deck
and
The Processing Deck

Coping Skills for Kids Workbook™

>>>>> MY SAD <<<<<
THERMOMETER

WHAT I LOOK LIKE

WHAT I CAN DO

BIG

MEDIUM

SMALL

WHAT MAKES YOU FEEL SAD?

 # WHAT MAKES OTHERS FEEL SAD?

PICK **1** COLOR AND **DRAW** ABOUT FEELING **SAD**.

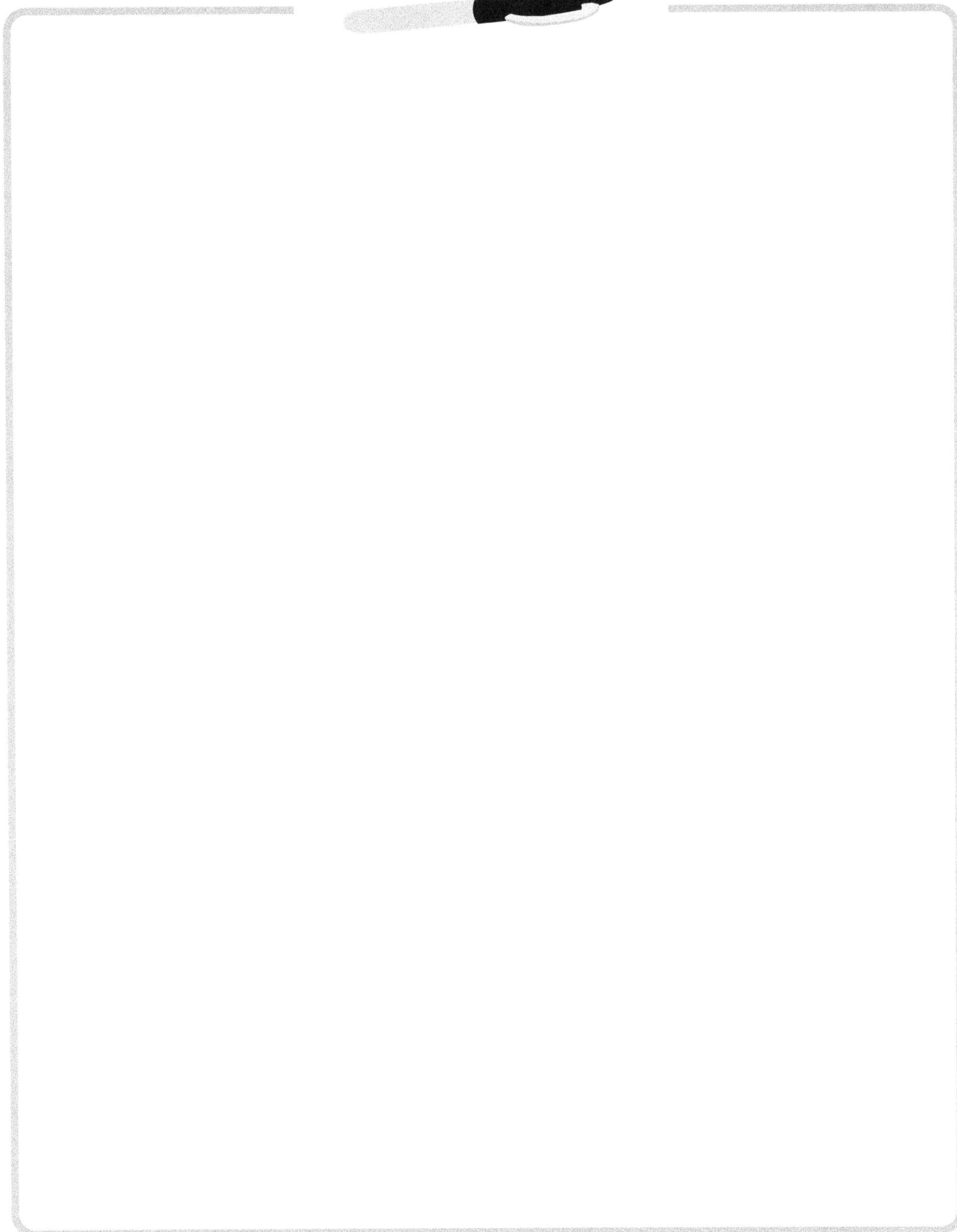

DRAW ABOUT FEELING SAD USING SHAPES.

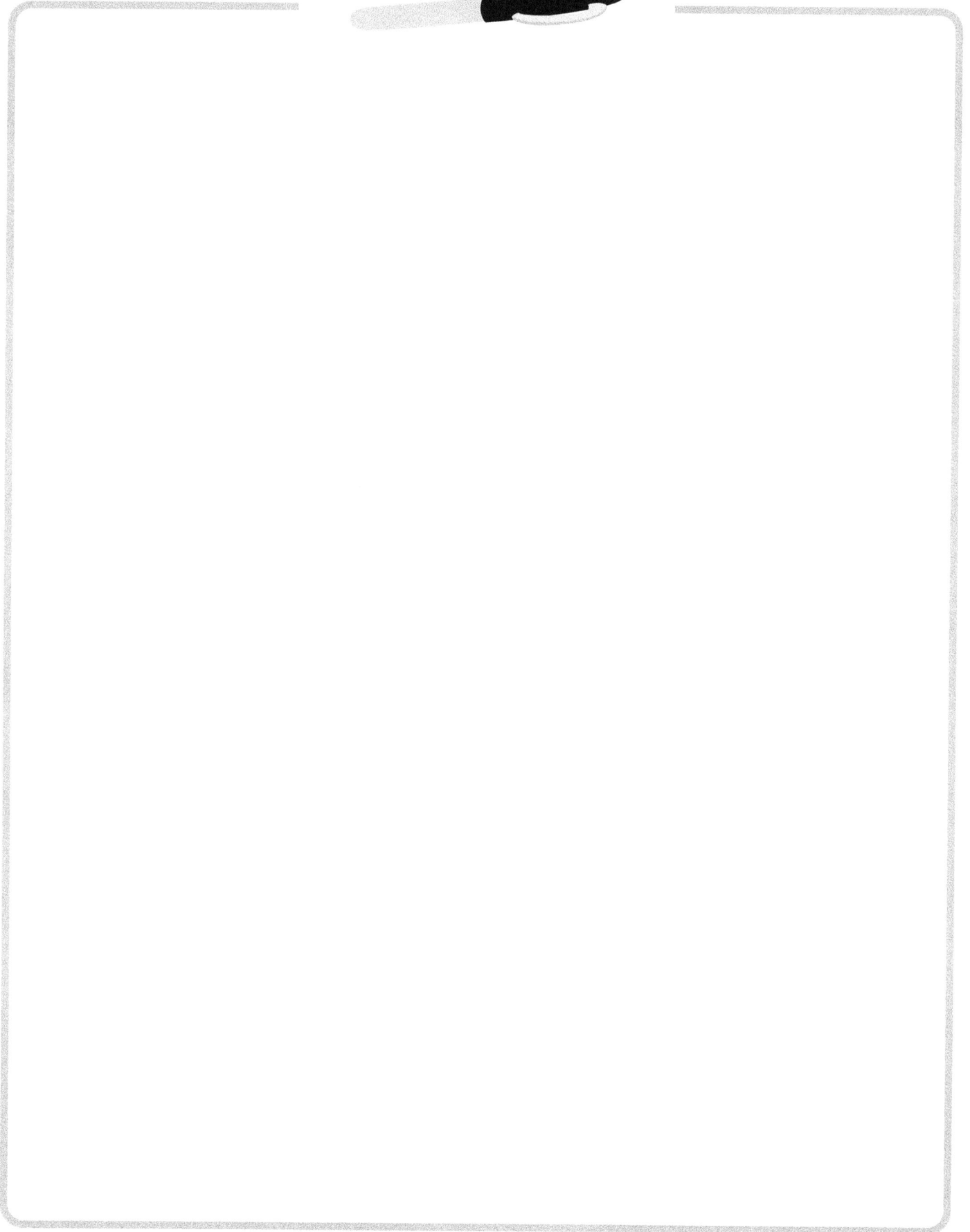

DRAW OR WRITE COPING SKILLS FOR FEELING SAD!

·MY FRUSTRATED·
THERMOMETER

WHAT I **LOOK** LIKE

WHAT I CAN **DO**

BIG

MEDIUM

SMALL

WHAT MAKES YOU FEEL FRUSTRATED?

 # WHAT MAKES OTHERS FEEL FRUSTRATED?

PICK 1 COLOR AND DRAW ABOUT FEELING FRUSTRATED.

DRAW ABOUT FEELING FRUSTRATED USING SHAPES.

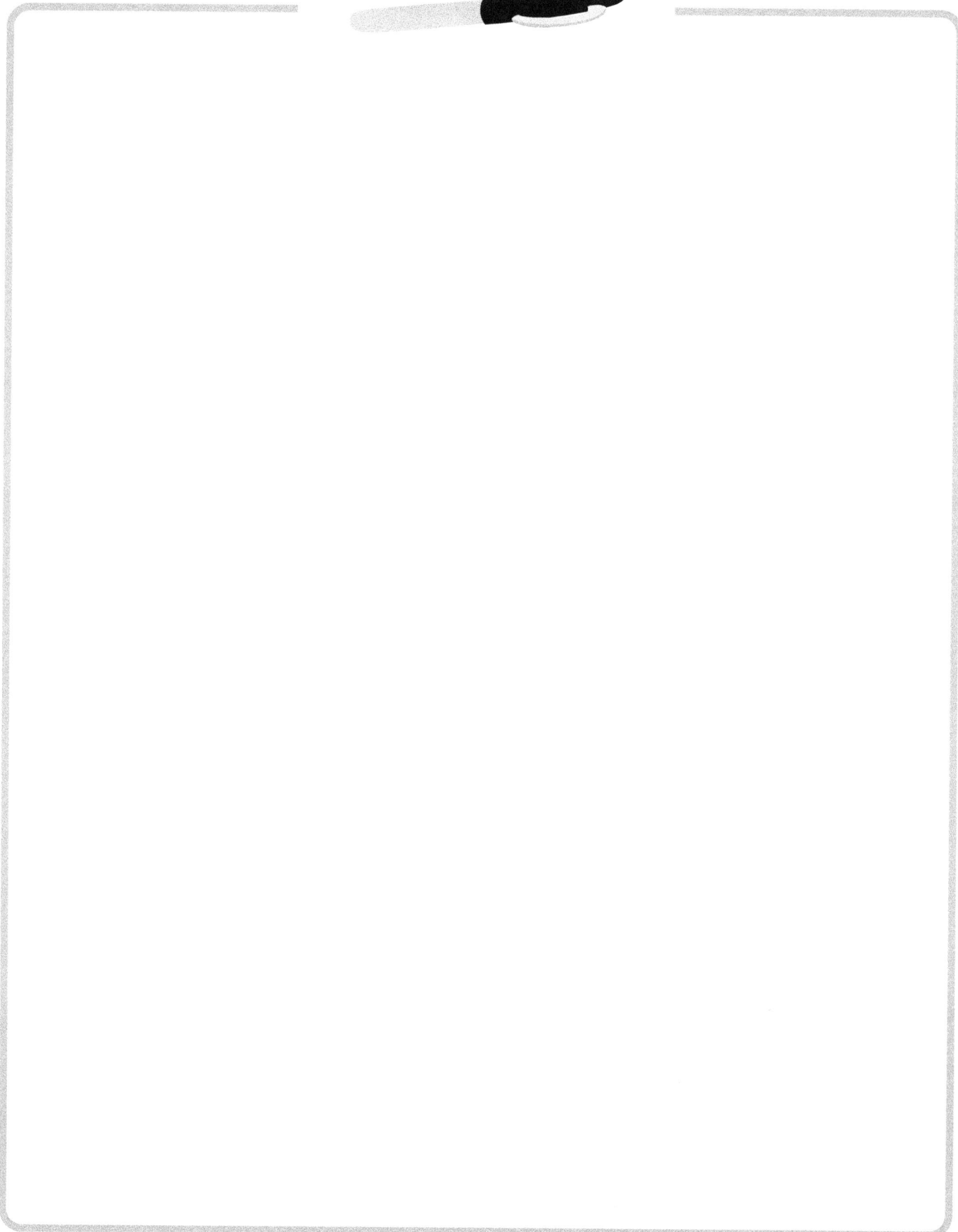

DRAW OR WRITE COPING SKILLS FOR FEELING FRUSTRATED!

MY MAD
THERMOMETER

WHAT I **LOOK** LIKE

WHAT I CAN **DO**

BIG

MED IUM

SMALL

WHAT MAKES YOU FEEL MAD?

WHAT MAKES OTHERS FEEL MAD?

PICK 1 COLOR AND DRAW ABOUT FEELING MAD.

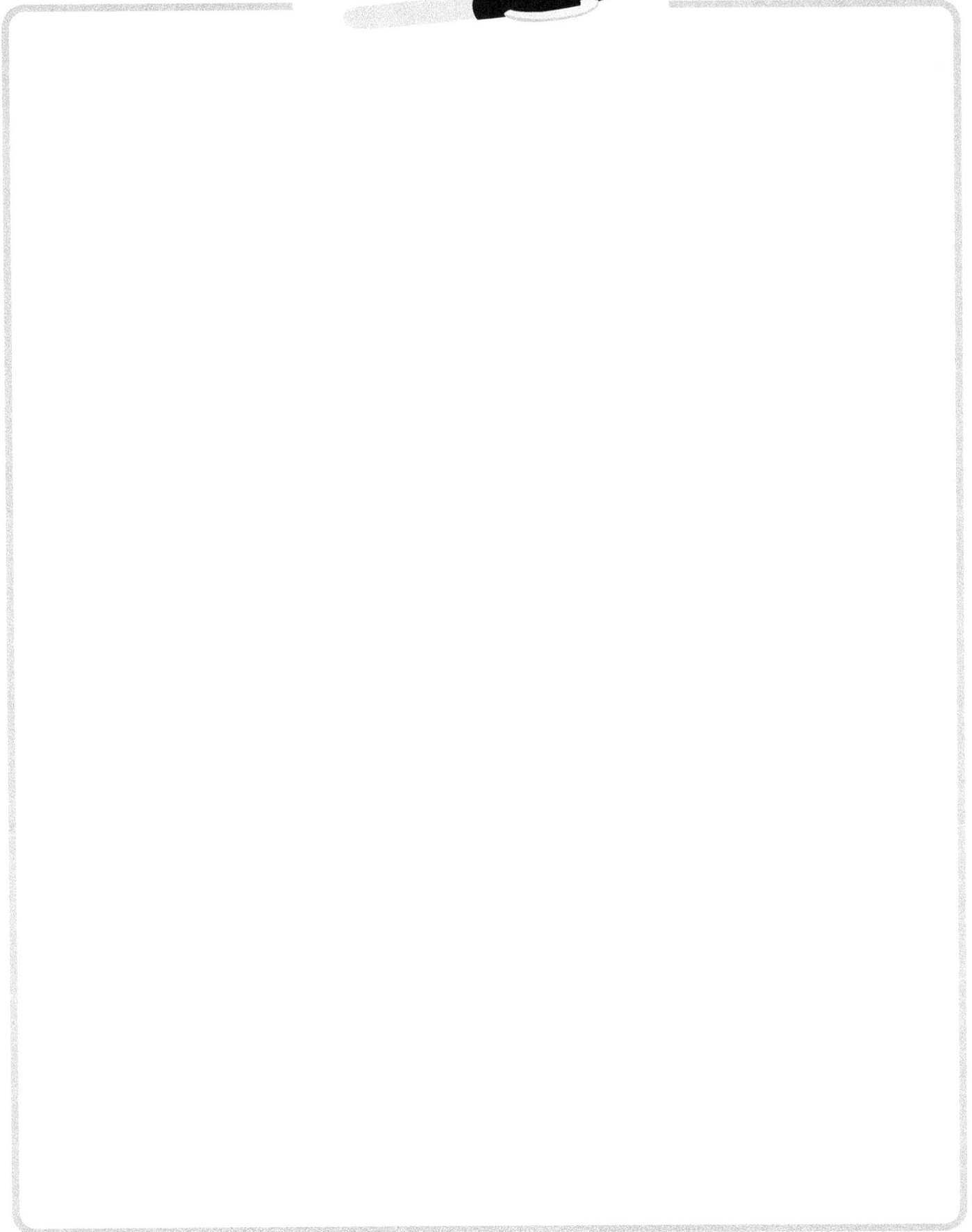

DRAW ABOUT FEELING **MAD** USING **SHAPES.**

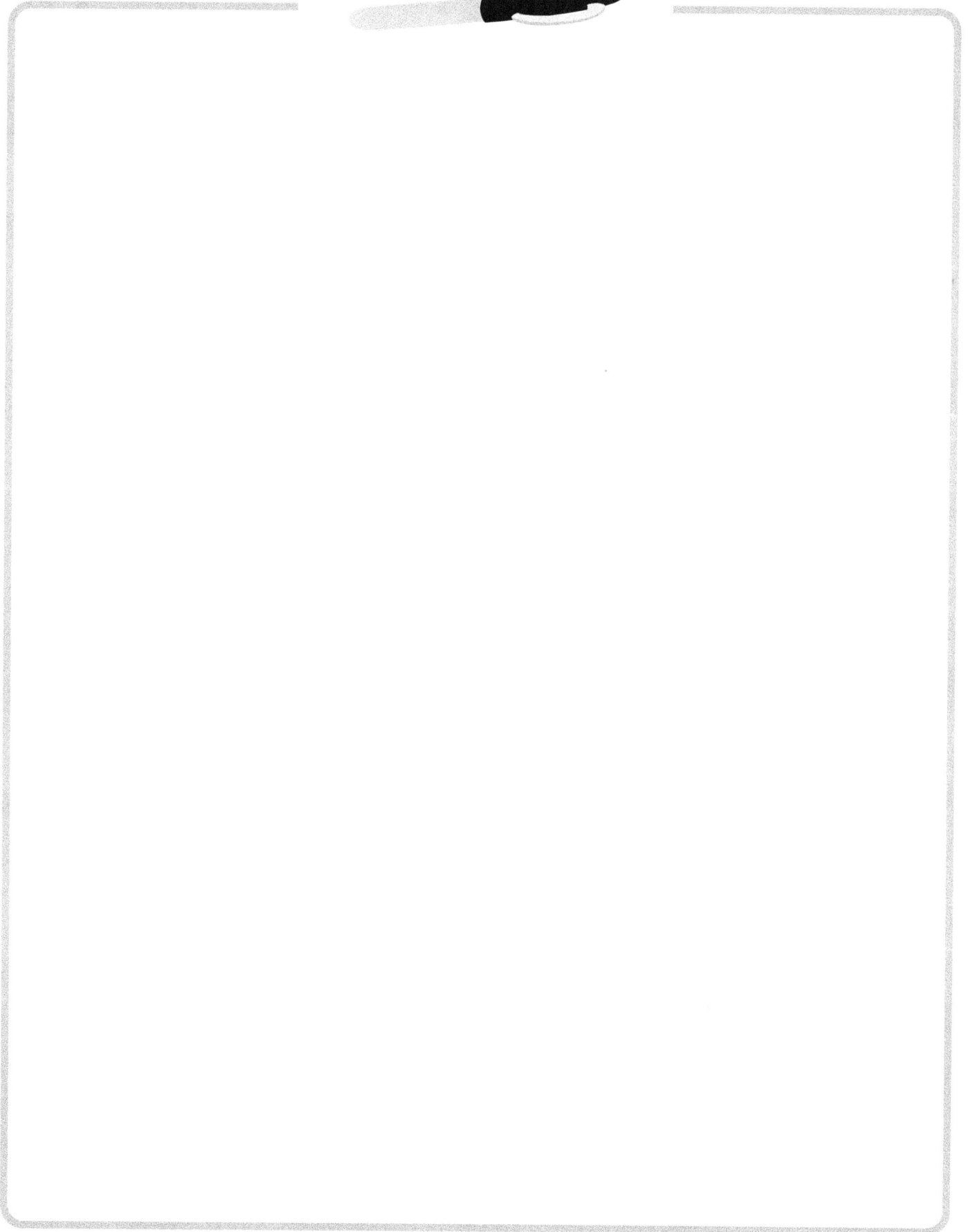

DRAW OR WRITE COPING SKILLS FOR FEELING MAD!

MY WORRIED THERMOMETER

WHAT I **LOOK** LIKE

WHAT I CAN **DO**

BIG

MED IUM

SMALL

WHAT MAKES YOU FEEL WORRIED?

WHAT MAKES OTHERS FEEL WORRIED?

PICK **1** COLOR AND **DRAW** ABOUT FEELING **WORRIED.**

DRAW ABOUT FEELING WORRIED USING SHAPES.

DRAW OR WRITE COPING SKILLS FOR FEELING WORRIED!

MY ANXIOUS
THERMOMETER

WHAT I **LOOK** LIKE

WHAT I CAN **DO**

BIG

MED IUM

SMALL

WHAT MAKES YOU FEEL ANXIOUS?

WHAT MAKES OTHERS FEEL ANXIOUS?

PICK 1 COLOR AND DRAW ABOUT FEELING ANXIOUS.

DRAW ABOUT FEELING ANXIOUS USING SHAPES.

DRAW OR WRITE COPING SKILLS FOR FEELING ANXIOUS!

MY OVERWHELMED THERMOMETER

WHAT I LOOK LIKE

WHAT I CAN DO

BIG

MED IUM

SMALL

WHAT MAKES YOU FEEL OVERWHELMED?

PICK **1** COLOR AND DRAW ABOUT FEELING OVERWHELMED.

DRAW ABOUT FEELING OVERWHELMED USING SHAPES.

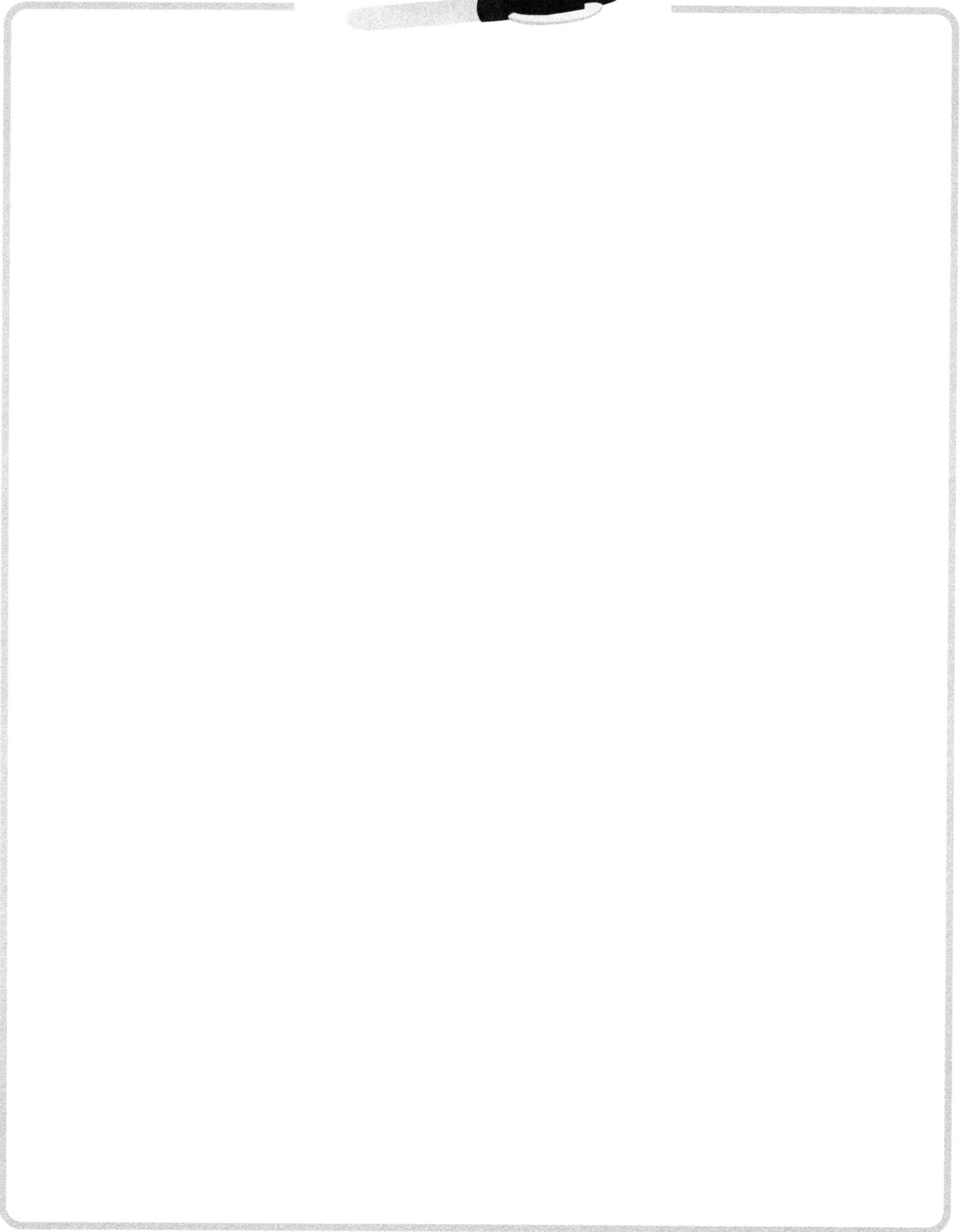

DRAW OR WRITE COPING SKILLS FOR FEELING OVERWHELMED!

MY SCARED THERMOMETER

WHAT I LOOK LIKE

WHAT I CAN DO

BIG

MEDIUM

SMALL

WHAT MAKES YOU FEEL SCARED?

WHAT MAKES OTHERS FEEL SCARED?

PICK **1** COLOR AND **DRAW** ABOUT FEELING **SCARED.**

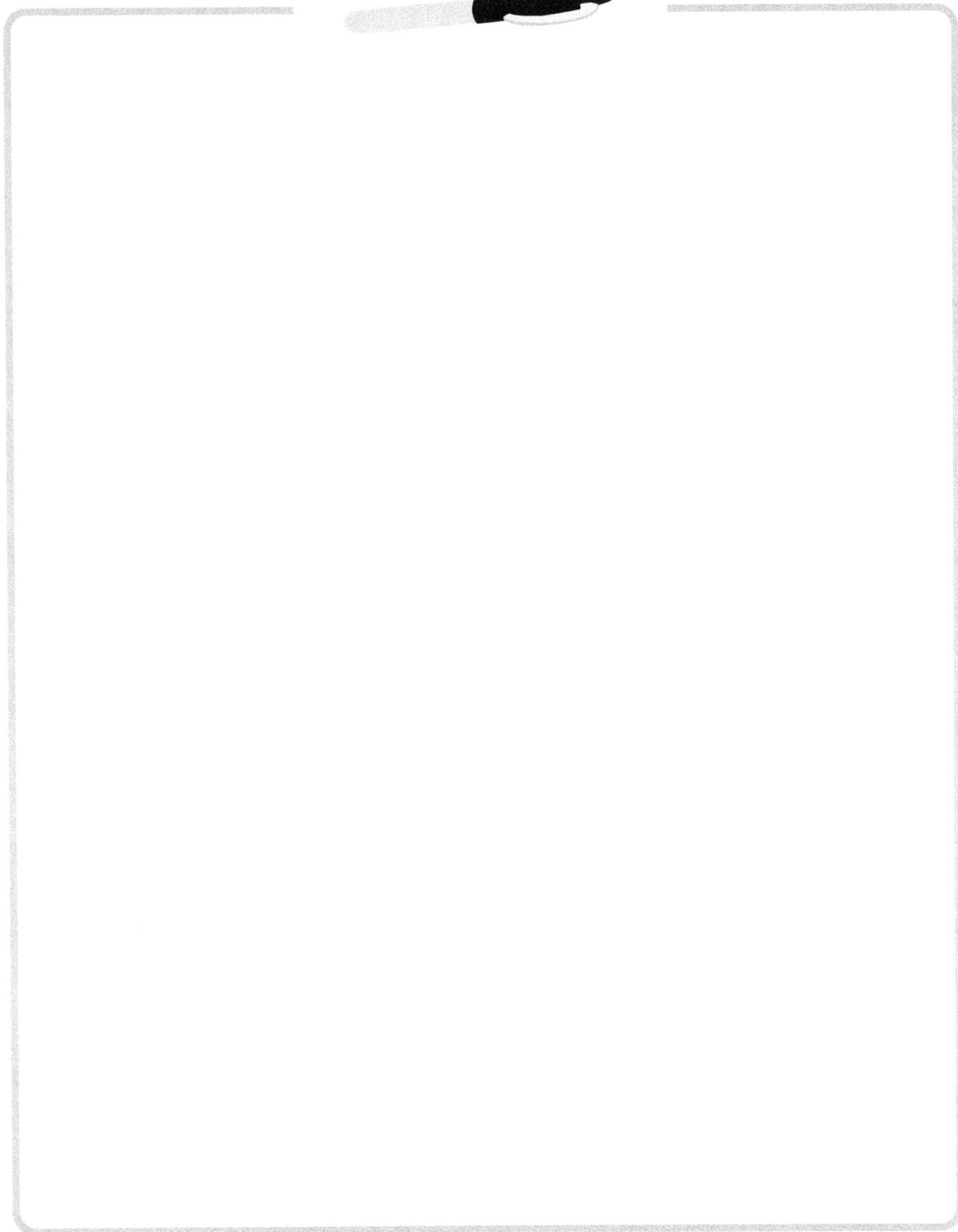

DRAW ABOUT FEELING SCARED USING SHAPES.

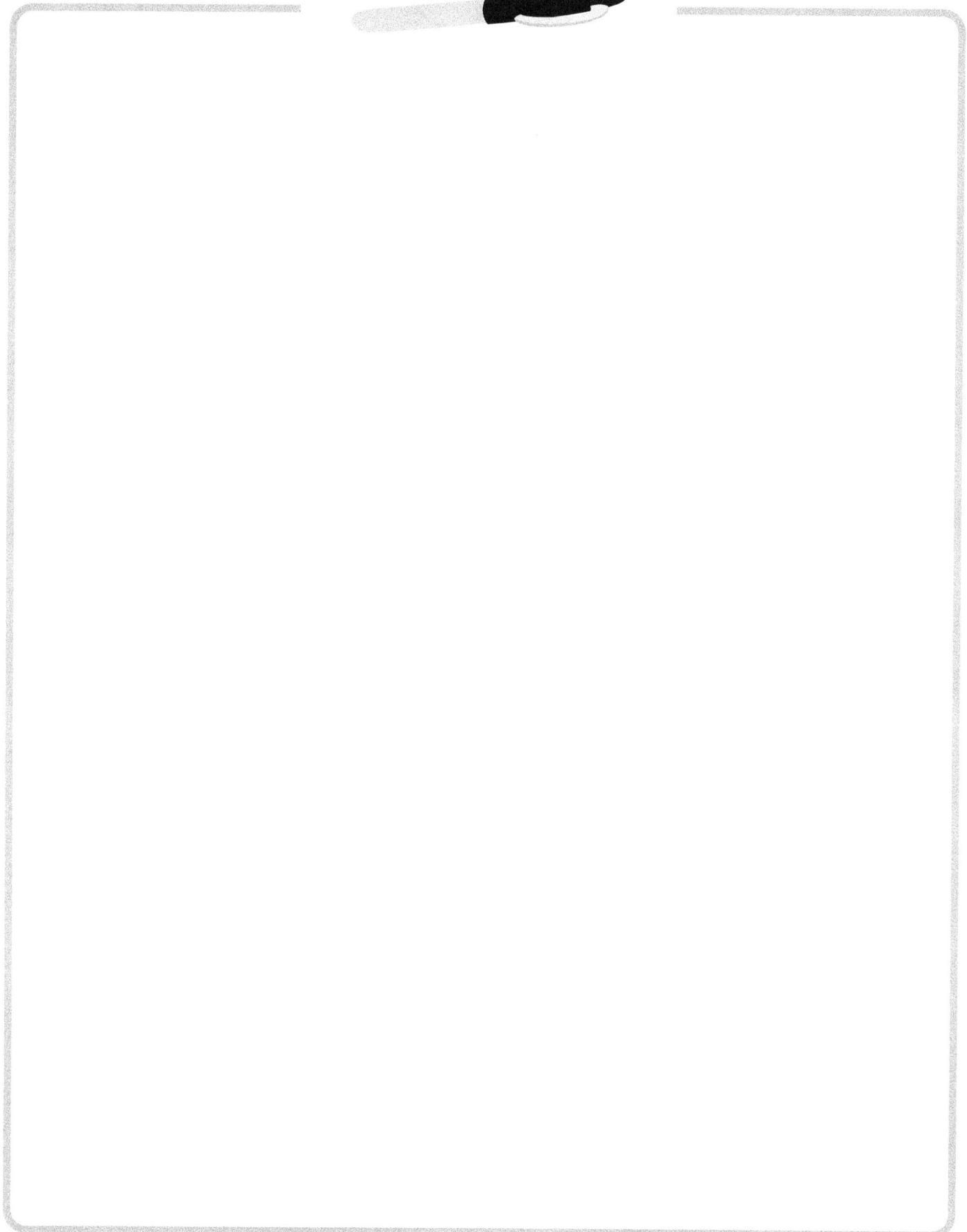

DRAW OR WRITE COPING SKILLS FOR FEELING SCARED!

MY EMBARRASSED THERMOMETER

WHAT I LOOK LIKE   WHAT I CAN DO

BIG

MEDIUM

SMALL

WHAT MAKES YOU FEEL EMBARRASSED?

 # WHAT MAKES OTHERS FEEL EMBARRASSED?

PICK **1** COLOR AND DRAW ABOUT FEELING EMBARRASSED.

DRAW ABOUT FEELING EMBARRASSED USING SHAPES.

DRAW OR WRITE COPING SKILLS FOR FEELING EMBARRASSED!

MY STRESSED THERMOMETER

WHAT I LOOK LIKE

WHAT I CAN DO

BIG

MEDIUM

SMALL

WHAT MAKES YOU FEEL STRESSED?

WHAT MAKES OTHERS FEEL STRESSED?

PICK **1** COLOR AND **DRAW** ABOUT FEELING **STRESSED.**

DRAW ABOUT FEELING STRESSED USING SHAPES.

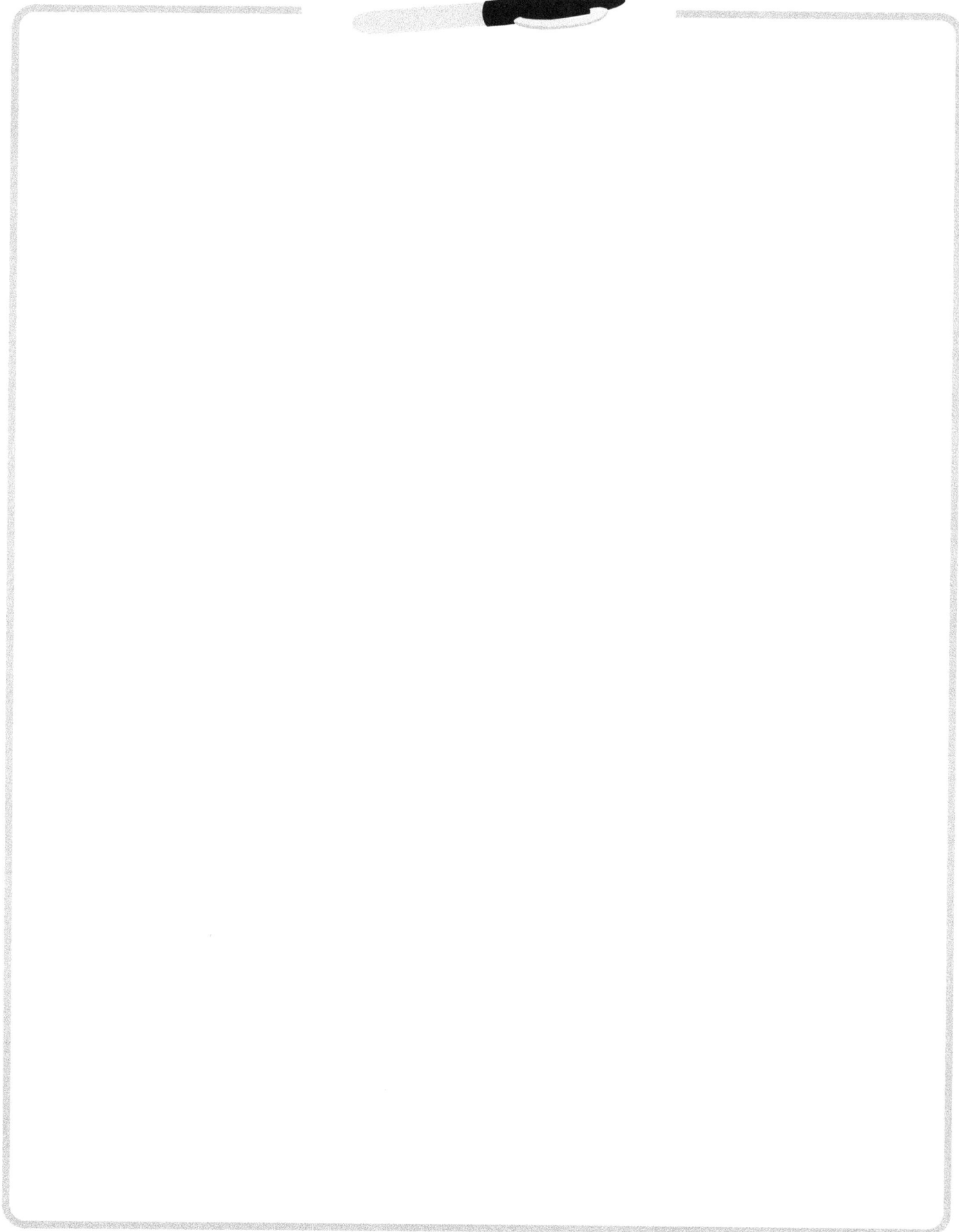

DRAW OR WRITE COPING SKILLS FOR FEELING STRESSED!

MY JEALOUS THERMOMETER

WHAT I LOOK LIKE

WHAT I CAN DO

BIG

MEDIUM

SMALL

WHAT MAKES YOU FEEL JEALOUS?

WHAT MAKES OTHERS FEEL JEALOUS?

PICK **1** COLOR AND **DRAW** ABOUT FEELING JEALOUS.

DRAW ABOUT FEELING JEALOUS USING SHAPES.

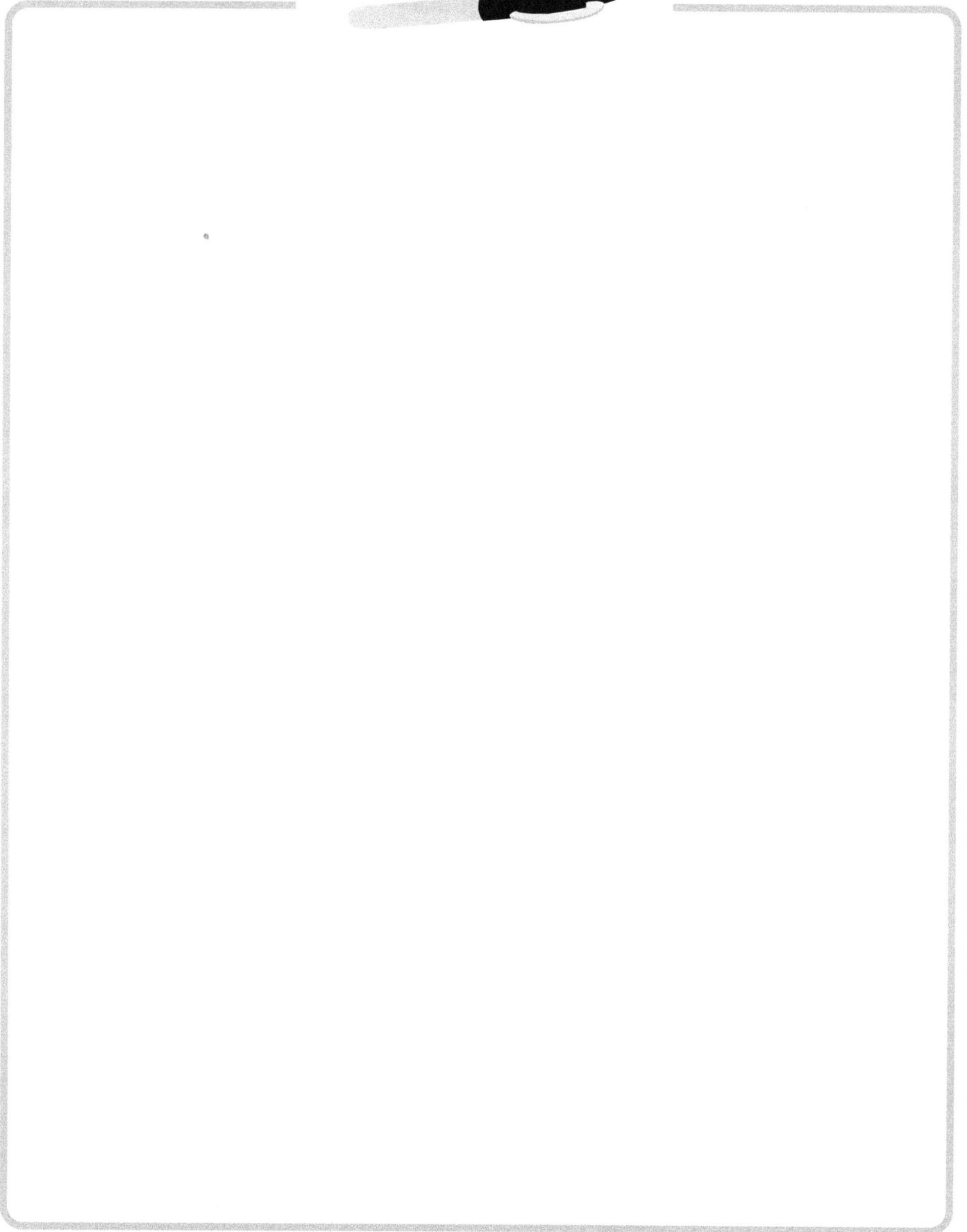

DRAW OR WRITE COPING SKILLS FOR FEELING JEALOUS!

MY THERMOMETER

WHAT I LOOK LIKE

WHAT I CAN DO

BIG

MEDIUM

SMALL

WHAT MAKES YOU FEEL _____?

WHAT MAKES OTHERS FEEL_____?

PICK 1 COLOR AND DRAW ABOUT FEELING _____.

DRAW ABOUT FEELING _____ USING SHAPES.

DRAW OR WRITE COPING SKILLS FOR FEELING _____!

THERMOMETER

WHAT I LOOK LIKE   WHAT I CAN DO

BIG

MEDIUM

SMALL

WHAT MAKES YOU FEEL _____?

WHAT MAKES OTHERS FEEL_____?

PICK 1 COLOR AND DRAW ABOUT FEELING _____.

DRAW ABOUT FEELING _____ USING SHAPES.

DRAW OR WRITE COPING SKILLS FOR FEELING_____!

HOW ARE YOU FEELING TODAY??

HOW ARE YOU FEELING TODAY? DRAW OR WRITE ABOUT IT!

HOW ARE YOU FEELING TODAY? DRAW OR WRITE ABOUT IT!

HOW ARE YOU FEELING TODAY? DRAW OR WRITE ABOUT IT!

HOW ARE YOU FEELING TODAY? DRAW OR WRITE ABOUT IT!

HOW ARE YOU FEELING TODAY? DRAW OR WRITE ABOUT IT!

HOW ARE YOU FEELING TODAY? DRAW OR WRITE ABOUT IT!

HOW ARE YOU FEELING TODAY? DRAW OR WRITE ABOUT IT!

HOW ARE YOU FEELING TODAY? DRAW OR WRITE ABOUT IT!

HOW ARE YOU FEELING TODAY? DRAW OR WRITE ABOUT IT!

HOW ARE YOU FEELING TODAY? DRAW OR WRITE ABOUT IT!

HOW ARE YOU FEELING TODAY? DRAW OR WRITE ABOUT IT!

HOW ARE YOU FEELING TODAY? DRAW OR WRITE ABOUT IT!

www.ingramcontent.com/pod-product-compliance
Lightning Source LLC
Chambersburg PA
CBHW081258040426
42452CB00014B/2552